DANCE ★ CRAZY

Mambo
& Merengue

Mambo
& Merengue

Paul Bottomer

LORENZ BOOKS

This edition first published by Lorenz Books

© Anness Publishing Limited 1997

Lorenz Books is an imprint of
Anness Publishing Limited
Hermes House
88–89 Blackfriars Road
London SE1 8HA

ISBN 1 85967 394 5

Publisher: Joanna Lorenz
Senior Editor: Lindsay Porter
Photographer: John Freeman
Clothes Stylist: Leeann Mackenzie
Hair and Make-up: Karen Kennedy
Designer: Siân Keogh

Printed in China

3 5 7 9 10 8 6 4 2

Contents

Mambo – an Introduction

The Mambo enjoys a rich past, originating in the fertile mixture of Afro-Caribbean and Latin American cultures found on the island of Cuba. Cuba had always been able to boast an amazing diversity of dances and rhythms. By the 1940s, a new and exciting sound, originally led by Odilio Urfé and Arsenio Rodriguez, was beginning to emerge. A mixture of Latin with a heavy Jazz influence, the style was developed by Dámaso Pérez Prado, a Cuban band leader based in Mexico who, by 1945, had turned it into the latest dance craze. This hot new dance, the Mambo, is believed to have been named after the voodoo priests who are able to send devotees into wild, hypnotic dances. The Mambo was initially condemned by the Church in some Latin American countries and restricted by the authorities in others. But, like any forbidden fruit, the Mambo gained in popularity and flourished.

By the 1950s, spurred on by Hollywood and the amazing popularity of Pérez "Prez" Prado, the Mambo had begun to establish itself as a favourite in the USA. Prado was one of the original "Mambo Kings", along with names like Tito Puente, Israel Lopez Cachao and the legendary Mambo musician Machito, all of whom performed at the famous Palladium in New York. They were joined by probably the greatest vocal interpreter of Mambo, Benny Moré. The singer Celia Cruz also became a Latin legend, but it was Prado's hits, such as "Mambo No. 5", "Mambo No. 8", "Mambo Jambo" and "Guaglione", that really brought the music and dance to explode onto the wider world dance scene to become the enduring favourite that it is today.

Left: Of Cuban origin, the Mambo is now enjoyed throughout the world at both social and competition levels.

Music and Rhythm

Mambo music is as fascinating as it is diverse. Like all Latin American dance music, the rhythm is exciting and for a dancer, the rhythm is the first concern. In Mambo, the rhythm is set by an astonishing variety of percussive instruments. These include the clave, two hardwood sticks which are tapped together; the guiro, which produces a rasping sound; maracas, originally hollow gourds filled with dried peas or small pebbles to make a rattle; the campana or cowbell; and a variety of drums, including the conga, tumba, bongo and timbales.

When first listening to Mambo music, it is not uncommon for the newcomer to be confused by the variety of rhythms within the umbrella of Mambo. This variety exists because Mambo marks a transition from several earlier dance rhythms into a distillation of all of them. In the same way as different chefs might produce the same dish but with variations according to each chef's preferences, so different musicians might produce one of the three different Mambo rhythms.

The first and simplest Mambo rhythm uses four basic beats, which a dancer will interpret as "Quick Quick Slow". This is the type of rhythm used in this book. The second type of

Right: This couple are preparing to dance an Underarm Turn, which can be mixed in an exotic cocktail of Mambo moves.

rhythm tends to be faster and uses the four basic beats which are interpreted as four "Quick" counts or "Quick Quick Slow" or the two are mixed together in one dance. This rhythm has largely become associated with Salsa. The third rhythm tends to be slower but splits beat four in half to produce three whole counts followed by two half counts. The two split beats followed by a whole beat give the familiar Cha Cha Cha rhythm. Although it may be interesting to understand what the rhythmic differences are and why they occur in the same dance, it is not necessary to delve too deeply into rhythm analysis in order to enjoy dancing the Mambo.

The tempo of Mambo music varies enormously, starting at about 32 bars per minute for Cha Cha Cha and rising to 40 for social dancing, before climaxing at a more challenging 56 bars per minute for expert dancers. Mambo music usually has a time signature of 4/4, which means that there are four equal beats to each bar of music, though 8/8 is also possible.

The Cuban Family of Dances

Fans of Latin American dancing often notice a similarity between the international styles of Mambo, Rumba, Cha Cha Cha and Salsa. This is because they all originate from the same Cuban source, finding their roots in the Bolero-Rumba, the Danzón and the Son.

The Rumba is a slow, sensuous and very beautiful dance of love. The pattern of the Cha Cha Cha moves has much in common with that of the Rumba but the speed is a little quicker and the mood is much more playful and teasing.

In Salsa, which is a distillation of many Latin and Afro-Caribbean dances, turns have become an important feature, so the overall look and feel are quite different from those of the Mambo, though the dances share many of the basic moves. In contrast to the Mambo, where the feel of the dance is generally based on forward and backward movements, Salsa moves have more of a side-to-side feel.

Mambo has a pattern, structure and feel which are closer to the Rumba and Cha Cha Cha, although it is a faster and more exuberant dance. The experienced Mambo dancer will use every beat of music and interpret them with four actions, comprising two steps, a movement of the foot in place and a final transfer of weight. In the international style of Mambo used in the introduction to the dance given in this book, three steps are danced over four beats of music. The steps themselves are simplified, so a "Quick" is danced to one beat and a "Slow" to two beats, following a normal pattern of "Quick Quick Slow".

There is a great technical debate about which action occurs on which beat. Experienced dancers often argue that the transfer of weight occurs on beat one, as has become the norm in the Rumba and Cha Cha Cha, while others maintain that it occurs on the final beat. In practice, dancers with a highly developed sense of formal technique tend to dance the weight transfer on count one, while social dancers and the Latins themselves tend to dance it on count four. Since both are possible, the dancer is entitled to dance to the emphasis of the beat given by the percussionists in any given musical arrangement. For the purposes of this book, the rhythm is that favoured by most social dancers, where Step 1 occurs on the first beat of the bar of music. Whatever the eventual outcome of the technical debate, no one can be wrong for simply getting onto the floor and enjoying dancing the Mambo.

Left: Mambo is one of the most exuberant of Cuban dances.

The Holds

In Mambo, several different holds will be used, depending on the figure being danced. Most starting figures are danced using a Close Contact Hold.

CLOSE CONTACT HOLD

The man and woman are in close contact. The man places his right hand well around the woman's waist with his right forearm across the small of the woman's back. The woman places her left hand on the man's upper right arm, right shoulder or the back of his neck. The man raises his left hand to just below shoulder level with his elbow away from his body. The woman then places the middle finger of her right hand between the thumb and first finger of the man's left hand. The man closes the fingers of his left hand to take hold.

The woman is positioned slightly to the man's right, so that his left foot is outside the woman's right foot when he moves forward onto his left foot and his right foot is between the woman's feet when he moves forward onto his right foot.

DOUBLE HAND HOLD

In this hold, the man and woman are a little apart. The man holds the

The Close Contact Hold seen from the front (left) and back (right).

woman's left hand in his right hand and her right hand in his left hand, just below shoulder height.

RIGHT HAND TO RIGHT HAND HOLD

This hold is very similar to shaking hands except that the man holds his hand palm upwards and the woman rests her palm on it. The hold should not be tight. The hands are held at about waist height. It is important for both the man's and woman's arms to be toned, but not rigid, to allow the man to give and the woman to receive the lead. What to do with the free arm depends on the move being danced and will be dealt with later in this book.

LEFT HAND TO RIGHT HAND HOLD

In this hold, you will be in an open position, a little apart from your partner. The man takes the woman's right hand in his left hand and the free arm is normally extended to the side at waist height.

RIGHT HAND TO LEFT HAND HOLD

This is the same as the hold above, but the woman's left hand is held in the man's right hand.

Basic Mambo

Even top dancers constantly return to the basic movements to rediscover the exciting simplicity of the unadorned dance. These moves perfectly characterize the Mambo's mood, personality and essence, and it is with these moves that we will begin. To start the dance, take up a Close Contact Hold. The man is standing with his weight on the right foot and the woman with her weight on the left foot.

1 Man
Move forward onto the left foot, leaving the right foot in place. (Count – quick)

2 Man
Transfer your body weight back onto the right foot. (Count – quick)

3 Man
Move back onto the left foot, a small step. (Count – slow)

1 Woman
Move back onto the right foot, leaving the left foot in place. (Count – quick)

2 Woman
Transfer your body weight forward onto the left foot. (Count – quick)

3 Woman
Move forward onto the right foot, a small step. (Count – slow)

4 Man

Move back onto the right foot, leaving the left foot in place. (Count – quick)

4 Woman

Move forward onto the left foot, leaving the right foot in place. (Count – quick)

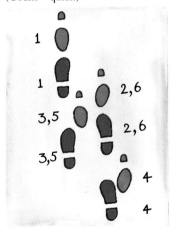

5 Man

Transfer your body weight forward onto the left foot. (Count – quick)

5 Woman

Transfer your body weight back onto the right foot. (Count – quick)

6 Man

Move forward onto the right foot, a small step. (Count – slow)

6 Woman

Move back onto the left foot, a small step. (Count – slow)

Feet and Legs

Throughout the Mambo, a forward movement is danced by pushing the body weight forward onto the ball of the foot and then lowering the heel. This is very different from a normal walk where the heel contacts the floor first. The action is very characteristic of Afro-Caribbean Latin American dancing, where no heels are used on forward movements. On a backward movement, the knee of the moving leg straightens as the body weight moves over the hip and the heel of the foot left in place is raised slightly from the floor. This action should not be exaggerated.

Due to the speed of the Mambo, it is often not possible to transfer all of the body weight onto the stepping foot. In this case, only part of the weight is used to give a feeling of pressure through the foot taking the step. On a sideways movement, the inside edge of the ball of the moving foot should contact the floor first and then the body weight is rolled over onto a flat foot as the heel is lowered. As the body weight moves onto the foot, the heel of the foot remaining in place is allowed to lift from the floor, leaving the inside edge of the ball of that foot in contact with the floor.

You can now repeat the Basic Mambo continuously or combine it with other moves described later in the book. Try gradually turning the Basic Mambo to the left, with a turn of no more than 90° to each set of six steps.

La Cucuracha

In Latin American Spanish, *cucuracha* means "cockroach", and is the name given to a move which is popular in several of the dances originating in Cuba. This compact move is a useful one to dance when the floor is crowded or while you are deciding what your next move will be. Start in a Close Contact Hold. The man is standing with his weight on the right foot and the woman with her weight on the left foot.

1 Man
Move sideways onto the left foot, leaving the right foot in place. (Count – quick)

1 Woman
Move sideways onto the right foot, leaving the left foot in place. (Count – quick)

2 Man
Transfer your body weight sideways onto the right foot. (Count – quick)

2 Woman
Transfer your body weight sideways onto the left foot. (Count – quick)

3 Man
Close the left foot to the right foot. (Count – slow)

3 Woman
Close the right foot to the left foot. (Count – slow)

Style Tip

As you move to the side on Steps 1 and 4 try to keep the upper part of your body relatively still, so that the sideways movement is achieved through your hips. If you find this a little tricky at first, a smaller step will help you to achieve the correct movement.

4 Man

Move sideways onto the right foot, leaving the left foot in place. (Count – quick)

5 Man

Transfer your body weight sideways onto the left foot. (Count – quick)

Dirty Mambo

With just two basic moves, you can already try out a new move by combining them in the Dirty Mambo. The Mambo received a great boost to its popularity when the feature film Dirty Dancing was released and this is probably how this figure got its name.

Dance Steps 1–3 of the Basic Mambo.
Dance Steps 4–6 of La Cucuracha.
Dance Steps 1–3 of La Cucuracha.
Dance Steps 4–6 of the Basic Mambo.

6 Man

Close the right foot to the left foot. (Count – slow)

6 Woman

Close the left foot to the right foot. (Count – slow)

4 Woman

Move sideways onto the left foot, leaving the right foot in place. (Count – quick)

5 Woman

Transfer your body weight sideways onto the right foot. (Count – quick)

After La Cucuracha, you can repeat the move or continue into the Basic Mambo or the Dirty Mambo.

Manita a Mano

Start this popular move in a Double Hand Hold. To do this, dance a complete Basic Mambo, started as usual in Close Contact Hold. During Steps 1–3 of the Basic Mambo, the man leads the woman to move away from him and releasing his right hand. During Steps 4–6 of the Basic Mambo, the man takes the woman's left hand in his right hand in a Double Hand Hold. The man is now standing on the right foot and woman on the left foot ready to dance Manita a Mano.

1 Man

Using your left hand, lead the woman's right side away from you and then release hold with your left hand. Move back onto the left foot, turning 90° to the left, into a side-by-side position with the woman and leaving the right foot in place. (Count – quick)

1 Woman

Move back onto the right foot, turning 90° to the right, into a side-by-side position with the man and leaving the left foot in place. (Count – quick)

2 Man

Transfer your body weight forward onto the right foot, starting to turn to the right. (Count – quick)

2 Woman

Transfer your body weight forward onto the left foot, starting to turn to the left. (Count – quick)

Style Tip

It is important to both the look and the feel of the Manita a Mano that, as the dancers step back into a side-by-side position, the elbows are away from the side of the body to avoid a cramped appearance.

3 Man

Move sideways onto the left foot to end facing the woman and resume a Double Hand Hold. (Count – slow)

4 Man

Using your right hand, lead the woman's left side away from you and then release hold with your right hand. Move back onto the right foot, turning 90° to the right, into a side-by-side position with the woman and leaving the left foot in place. (Count – quick)

5 Woman

Transfer your body weight forward onto the right foot, starting to turn to the right. (Count – quick)

6 Man

Move sideways onto the right foot to end facing the woman and resume a Double Hand Hold. (Count – slow)

4 Woman

Move back onto the left foot, turning 90° to the left, into a side-by-side position with the man and leaving the right foot in place. (Count – quick)

3 Woman

Move sideways onto the right foot to end facing the man and resume a Double Hand Hold. (Count – slow)

5 Man

Transfer your body weight forward onto the left foot, starting to turn to the left. (Count – quick)

6 Woman

Move sideways onto the left foot to end facing the man and resume a Double Hand Hold. (Count – slow)

7–9 Man & Woman

Repeat Steps 1–3.

Continue into Steps 4–6 of the Basic Mambo, resuming Close Contact Hold, or try the Underarm Spot Turn to the Right.

Underarm Spot Turn to the Right

The move gives a nice finish to a wide variety of figures. It can end in any hold, it is also a great figure to use in preparing for a move which requires a change of hold. You can dance this turn after Steps 1–3 of the Basic Mambo but, for now, assume that you have just danced Manita a Mano. The man is standing on the left foot and the woman on the right foot. Both have their feet apart and are in a Double Hand Hold. On the last step of Manita a Mano, the man should raise his left hand and release his right hand to indicate the turn. While the woman dances the Spot Turn, the man's steps are the same as Steps 4–6 of the Basic Mambo, but ending with a short side step.

1 Man

Move back onto the right foot, leaving the left foot in place. Lead the turn by moving your raised hand to the left. (Count – quick)

1 Woman

On the right foot, swivel 90° to the right and move forward under the man's raised hand onto the left foot, leaving the right foot in place. Once on the left foot, swivel 180° to the right to end with the left foot back. The right foot is still in place and the man is on your right. (Count – quick)

2 Man

Transfer your body weight forward onto the left foot. (Count – quick)

2 Woman

Transfer your body weight forward onto the right foot, starting to turn to the right towards the man. (Count – quick)

3 Man

Move sideways onto the right foot, a small step, lowering your left arm. (Count – slow)

3 Woman

Move sideways onto the left foot, turning to the right to face the man. (Count – slow)

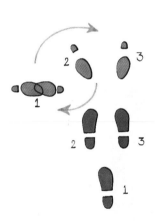

In a Close Contact Hold, you can now continue with the Basic Mambo or La Cucuracha. In a Double Hand Hold, you can continue with another Manita a Mano or the New York, a figure which opens up further possibilities.

The Free Arm

In Mambo, as in most Latin American dances, there are many moves in which the man and woman are holding with only one hand. By following some general guidelines about what to do with your free arm and hand, you can give your dance a superb appearance and a balanced feel.

• During a movement, the position of the free arm and hand should mirror the height and curve of the joined arm and hand. It is neater to avoid spreading the fingers.

• During a turn on the spot, the arm should be drawn out of the way across the body and then allowed to return naturally to its position mirroring the joined hand and arm.

• The free arm should never be held above shoulder height nor dropped to the side, as this not only looks bad but severely inhibits good balance.

As you develop a feel for the dance, you may wish to respond by moving the free arm in a natural, balanced and gentle way. Do not exaggerate the movements, and match not only your own movements but also those of your partner. As Mambo is one of the livelier Latin American dances, it is a good idea to keep the free arm relatively still in relation to your body. A still arm has the effect of enhancing the appearance of the leg and hip action.

New York

Many of the developments in the Mambo took place in the Hispanic barrios, or neighbourhoods, of New York, so it is entirely appropriate that this move should be named after that great melting-pot of music and dance styles. To dance the New York, start in a Double Hand Hold, having just danced either the Basic Mambo or the Underarm Spot Turn to the Right. As a contrasting variation, you can also start the New York after Step 6 of the Manita a Mano. The man is standing on the right foot and the woman on the left foot.

1 Man
Release hold with the right hand and draw the left hand across and forward, swivelling 90° to the right on the right foot. Move forward onto the left foot, leaving the right foot in place. (Count – quick)

1 Woman
Release hold with the left hand and swivel 90° to the left on the left foot. Move forward onto the right foot, leaving the left foot in place. (Count – quick)

2 Man
Transfer your body weight back onto the right foot. (Count – quick)

2 Woman
Transfer your body weight back onto the left foot. (Count – quick)

3 Man
Swivel 90° to the left on the right foot and move sideways onto the left foot to face the woman. (Count – slow)

3 Woman
Swivel 90° to the right on the left foot and move sideways onto the right foot to face the man. Resume a Double Hand Hold. (Count – slow)

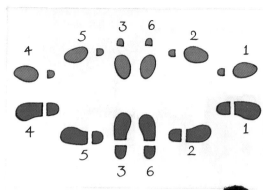

4 Man

Release hold with the left hand and draw the right hand across and forward, swivelling 90° to the left on the left foot. Move forward onto the right foot, leaving the left foot in place. (Count – quick)

4 Woman

Release hold with the right hand and swivel 90° to the right on the right foot. Move forward onto the left foot, leaving the right foot in place. (Count – quick)

5 Man

Transfer your body weight back onto the left foot. (Count – quick)

5 Woman

Transfer your body weight back onto the right foot. (Count – quick)

6 Man

Swivel 90° to the right on the left foot and move sideways onto the right foot to face the woman. Resume a Double Hand Hold but do not grip. (Count – slow)

6 Woman

Swivel 90° to the left on the right foot and move sideways onto the left foot to face the man. Resume a Double Hand Hold. (Count – slow)

You are now in a position to continue with the Basic Mambo, resuming a Close Contact Hold. When you feel confident, dance Steps 1–3 again and follow straight into the Underarm Spot Turn to the Right. Another fabulous combination is to dance the six steps of the New York and then follow with Underarm Spot Turns to the Right and the Left.

Underarm Spot Turn to the Left

This is the mirror image of the Underarm Spot Turn to the Right and is not only a useful figure to have in your repertoire but also looks spectacular when combined with the Underarm Spot Turn to the Right. Start in a Double Hand Hold. The man is standing on the right foot and the woman on the left foot. On the last step of the previous move, the man will raise his left hand and release hold with his right hand to indicate the turn.

1 Man
Move back onto the left foot leaving the right foot in place. Lead the turn by moving your raised hand to the right. (Count – quick)

1 Woman
On the left foot, swivel 90° to the left and move forward under the man's raised hand onto the right foot, leaving the left foot in place. Once on the right foot, swivel 180° to the left to end with the right foot back. The left foot is still in place and the man is on your left. (Count – quick)

2 Man
Transfer your body weight forward onto the right foot. (Count – quick)

2 Woman
Transfer your body weight forward onto the left foot, starting to turn to the left towards the man. (Count – quick)

3 Man
Move sideways onto the left foot, a small step, lowering your hand. (Count – slow)

3 Woman
Move sideways onto the right foot, turning to the left to face the man. (Count – slow)

Continue into Steps 4–6 of the Basic Mambo, taking up a Close Contact Hold.

New York Bus Stop

With a little imagination and know-how, basic moves can be combined and developed to great effect. Here is an easy variation of the New York which has a fun surprise element. To set up the move, begin by dancing the New York. You are now in Double Hand Hold. The man is standing on the right foot and the woman on the left foot. Note the change of rhythm.

1 Man
Release hold with the right hand and draw the left hand across and forward, swivelling 90° to the right on the right foot. Move forward onto the left foot, leaving the right foot in place. (Count – quick)

2 Man
Transfer your body weight back onto the right foot. (Count – quick)

3 Man
Swivel 90° to the left on the right foot and move sideways, a small step, onto the left foot to face the woman, leaving the right foot in place. Resume a Double Hand Hold but do not grip. (Count – quick)

1 Woman
Release hold with the left hand and swivel 90° to the left on the left foot. Move forward onto the right foot, leaving the left foot in place. (Count – quick)

2 Woman
Transfer your body weight back onto the left foot. (Count – quick)

3 Woman
Swivel 90° to the right on the left foot and move sideways onto the right foot to face the man, leaving the left foot in place. Resume a Double Hand Hold. (Count – quick)

4 Man

Transfer your body weight onto the right foot.
(Count – quick)

5 Man

Release hold with the right hand and draw the left hand across and forward, swivelling 90° to the right on the right foot. Move forward onto the left foot, leaving the right foot in place. (Count – quick)

5 Woman

Release hold with the left hand and swivel 90° to the left on the left foot. Move forward onto the right foot, leaving the left foot in place.
(Count – quick)

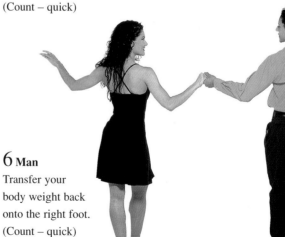

6 Man

Transfer your body weight back onto the right foot.
(Count – quick)

4 Woman

Transfer your body weight onto the left foot.
(Count – quick)

6 Woman

Transfer your body weight back onto the left foot. (Count – quick)

7 Man

Swivel 90° to the left on the right foot and move sideways onto the left foot to face the woman, leaving the right foot in place. Resume a Double Hand Hold but do not grip. (Count – slow)

7 Woman

Swivel 90° to the right on the left foot and move sideways onto the right foot to face the man, leaving the left foot in place. Resume a Double Hand Hold. (Count – slow)

El Mambo Mexicano

For ease of communication, it is often simpler to give a particular combination its own name. Let's call this one El Mambo Mexicano. This very simple but effective combination can be slipped into your programme after a little practice. It looks impressive and only you will know that it is not as complicated as it appears!

• Underarm Spot Turn to the Right, ending in a Right Hand to Right Hand Hold (maintain this hold throughout the rest of the combination)
• Basic Mambo
• Steps 1–3 of the New York
• Steps 4–6 of the Basic Mambo (the backward half)
• Steps 1–3 of the Basic Mambo (the forward half)
• Steps 4–6 of the New York
• Steps 1–3 of the Basic Mambo (the forward half)
• Underarm Spot Turn to the Right, resuming normal Close Contact Hold on Step 3

8–14 Man & Woman

Repeat Steps 1–7, in the opposite direction and using the opposite feet and hands.

You are now in the right position to continue with the Basic Mambo or any other appropriate figure you have learned. The New York Bus Stop can be used to good effect in combination with the New York: dance a complete New York, then Steps 1–7 of the New York Bus Stop, Steps 4–6 then Steps 1–3 of the New York, and finally Steps 8–14 of the New York Bus Stop.

La Peonza

*P*eonza means a toy spinning top. While not as vigorous as the name suggests, this move brings the couple together in a Close Contact Hold to turn clockwise around a central point between them. The amount of turn can be varied according to conditions on the floor and it is a good move to help you find a clear space for your next move. La Peonza is an easy figure to dance and, since it takes up no space, it is useful on a crowded floor as the temperature rises with the soaring trumpets of the hot Mambo music. The man and woman close and open their feet alternately to help maintain the turn.

1 Man
Close the right foot to the left foot.
(Count – quick)

2 Man
Move sideways onto the left foot.
(Count – quick)

1 Woman
Move sideways onto the left foot.
(Count – quick)

2 Woman
Close the right foot to the left foot.
(Count – quick)

La Peonza with Underarm Spot Turn to the Left

In a very attractive development of this figure, the man can lead the woman to dance an Underarm Spot Turn to the Left during Steps 4–6 of La Peonza by raising his left hand on Step 3 and moving it to the right. The man continues to dance his normal La Peonza steps, curving his right arm around, but not necessarily in contact with, the woman's waist. The couple resume the normal moves of La Peonza on Steps 7–9.

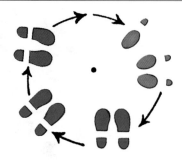

3 Man ▶

Close the right foot to
the left foot. (Count –
slow)

3 Woman

Move sideways onto
the left foot. (Count
– slow)

4–8 Man

Move sideways onto
the left foot. Close the
right foot to the left
foot. Move sideways
onto the left foot.
Close the right foot to
the left foot. Move
sideways onto the left
foot. (Counts – quick,
quick, slow, quick,
quick)

4–8 Woman

Close the right foot to
the left foot. Move
sideways onto the left
foot. Close the right
foot to the left foot.
Move sideways onto
the left foot. Close the
right foot to the left
foot. (Counts – quick,
quick, slow, quick,
quick)

9 Man

Close the right foot to
the left foot. (Count –
slow)

9 Woman

Move sideways
onto the left foot.
(Count – slow)

Style Tip

Use a Merengue action (see the Merengue
section of the book) as you dance steps
1–8 of La Peonza.

*Continue with the Basic Mambo, La
Cucuracha or another appropriate figure.*

El Contro Cuerpo

"El sentimiento es mas importante que las figuras" ("The feeling is more important than the figures") is a good axiom for all dancers. El Contro Cuerpo (or "The Cross Body Basic") is a superb but simple move in which the dancers can really start to work with each other's body weight to generate that all-important feeling of dancing with your partner in a physical relationship. It is also a super floorcraft move for quickly changing your orientation through 180° to find new space on the floor and new opportunities to enjoy your figures. Start in a Close Contact Hold. The man is standing on the right foot and the woman on the left foot.

1 Man

Move forward onto the left foot, leaving the right foot in place. (Count – quick)

2 Man

Transfer your body weight back onto the right foot. (Count – quick)

3 Man

Turning 90° to the left, move sideways onto the left foot and bring your left hand down towards your left hip. (Count – slow)

1 Woman

Move back onto the right foot, leaving the left foot in place. (Count – quick)

2 Woman

Transfer your body weight forward onto the left foot. (Count – quick)

3 Woman

Move forward onto the right foot, starting to move across the man. (Count – slow)

4 Man

Move back onto the right foot, a short step, leaving the left foot in place. (Count – quick)

5 Man

Transfer your body weight forward onto the left foot. (Count – quick)

6 Man

On the left foot, swivel 90° to the left and move diagonally forward onto the right foot to end facing the woman. Raise the left hand to normal height. (Count – slow)

4 Woman

Move forward onto the left foot across the man. (Count – quick)

5 Woman

Move forward onto the right foot across the man, leaving the left foot in place. On the right foot, swivel 180° to the left to end with the right foot back. (Count – quick)

6 Woman

Move diagonally back, a short step, onto the left foot. (Count – slow)

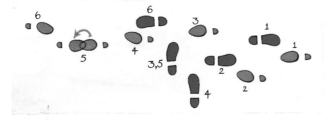

At the end of the move, take up the hold appropriate to your next figure. Now repeat the move or continue with the Basic Mambo and La Peonza, the Underarm Spot Turn to the Left or another appropriate figure, such as the Manhattan.

Manhattan

The Manhattan is a stylish move in which the man leads the woman by actually showing her what to do and then leading her through the move. Then the woman takes her turn to dance the man's steps as the whole move is repeated. To dance the Manhattan, the couple are in a Double Hand Hold. The man is standing on the right foot and the woman on the left foot.

1 Man
Move back onto the left foot, leaving the right foot in place. (Count – quick)

1 Woman
Move back onto the right foot, leaving the left foot in place. (Count – quick)

2 Man
Transfer your body weight forward onto the right foot, raising your left arm above your own head and starting to turn to the right underneath it. (Count – quick)

2 Woman
Transfer your body weight forward onto the left foot. (Count – quick)

3 Man
Continue turning to complete a 180° turn to the right, ending in a side-by-side position and moving back onto the left foot. Lower your left hand to waist height (shown here from the front). (Count – slow)

3 Woman
Close the right foot to the left foot (shown here from the front). (Count – slow)

4 Man

Move back onto the right foot, leaving the left foot in place. Release hold with the right hand. (Count – quick)

4 Woman

Move forward onto the left foot, leaving the right foot in place. (Count – quick)

5 Man

Transfer your body weight forward onto the left foot. (Count – quick)

5 Woman

Move forward onto the right foot, leaving the left foot in place. On the right foot, swivel 180° to the left to end with the right foot back. (Count – quick)

6 Man

Move forward onto the right foot, a small step, resuming Double Hand Hold. (Count – slow)

6 Woman

Move back onto the left foot, a small step. (Count – slow)

7 Man

Move back onto the left foot, leaving the right foot in place. (Count – quick)

7 Woman

Move back onto the right foot, leaving the left foot in place. (Count – quick)

8 Man

Transfer your body weight forward onto the right foot. (Count – quick)

8 Woman

Transfer your body weight forward onto the left foot. (Count – quick)

Manhattan Cocktail

The Manhattan can easily be adapted to feature both the man and the woman in a cocktail of Manhattan moves. Dance the Manhattan as described with the woman dancing the man's steps the second time round. By omitting Steps 7–9 in the first Manhattan, the man can dance it again. By omitting Steps 7–9 in the second Manhattan, the woman can dance it again. Have fun working out other variations and mixing your own cocktail.

9 Man

Close the left foot to the right foot. (Count – slow)

9 Woman

Close the right foot to the left foot. (Count – slow)

The Manhattan continues with the woman dancing the man's steps and the man dancing the woman's steps. Resume your programme by dancing the Basic Mambo, moving into a Close Contact Hold, or any other appropriate figure.

El Molinito

El Molinito (the "Little Windmill") is actually a combination of moves, which when put together, give a special effect. This is due mainly to the interesting use of the arms and the relative positions of the man and woman as they progress through the moves. It is easier to work through this group in sections.

UNDERARM SPOT TURN TO THE RIGHT, OVERTURNED TO A SIDE-BY-SIDE POSITION

1 Man
Raising your left hand to initiate the woman's turn, move back onto the right foot, leaving the left foot in place. (Count – quick)

2 Man
Transfer your body weight forward onto the left foot, continuing to turn the woman clockwise. (Count – quick)

1 Woman
On the right foot, swivel 90° to the right and move forward under the man's raised hand onto the left foot, leaving the right foot in place. Once on the left foot, swivel 180° to the right to end with the left foot back. The right foot is still in place and the man is on your right. (Count – quick)

2 Woman
Transfer your body weight forward onto the right foot, starting to turn to the right towards the man. (Count – quick)

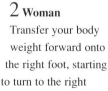

3 Man

Close the right foot to the left foot, leading the woman to continue turning, to end with her back to you on your right side. Place the woman's right hand in your right hand and take it over her head to end with your right arm across her shoulders and your right hand holding her right hand on her right shoulder. Take hold of the woman's left hand with your left hand. (Count – slow)

EL MOLINITO

4 Man

Move forward onto the left foot, raising your right hand a little over the woman's head as she moves back. (Count – quick)

5 Man

Move sideways onto the right foot, retaining hold with the right hand but releasing the left hand. (Count – quick)

3 Woman

Move forward onto the left foot towards the man's right side, turning to the right to face the man. On the left foot, continue to turn by swivelling 180° to the right to end facing in the same direction as the man, on his right side. (Count – slow)

4 Woman

Bending forward from the waist underneath the man's arm, move back onto the right foot, retaining hold with the right hand and releasing hold with the left hand. (Count – quick)

5 Woman

Move sideways onto the left foot, retaining hold with the right hand and resuming a normal upright stance. (Count – quick)

6 Man

Close the left foot to the right foot, taking hold of the woman's left hand in your left hand on your left side. (Count – slow)

6 Woman

Move forward onto the right foot to the man's left side, allowing the man to take hold of your left hand with his left hand. (Count – slow)

7 Man

Move back onto the right foot, releasing hold with your right hand and raising your left hand to allow the woman to pass underneath it. (Count – quick)

7 Woman

Move forward onto the left foot underneath your raised left hand. (Count – quick)

8 Man

Move sideways onto the left foot. (Count – quick)

8 Woman

Move sideways onto the right foot underneath the raised arms. (Count – quick)

9 Man

Move forward onto the right foot to the woman's left side. Place your right hand either around the woman's waist or on her right shoulder blade. (Count – slow)

9 Woman

Close the left foot to the right foot. (Count – slow)

LA CUCURACHA

10–12 Man
Dance La Cucuracha to the left. (Counts – quick, quick, slow)

10–12 Woman
Dance La Cucuracha to the right. (Counts – quick, quick, slow)

EXIT

13–15 Man & Woman
The man releases hold with the right hand. Dance Steps 4–6 of the Manhattan, the man leading the woman to turn to her left to face him before releasing hold with his left hand and resuming a normal Close Contact Hold. (Counts – quick, quick, slow)

The Liquidizer

D on't worry. "The Liquidizer" is just a fun name for a move with a rather longer technically descriptive title. In this series of moves, the man and woman move around each other, hence the Liquidizer. This figure is not difficult but will require a little practice to ensure that the man and woman maintain a good orientation to each other. The result will be simple but spectacular. Start the move by dancing Steps 1–3 of El Contro Cuerpo with a Right Hand to Right Hand Hold. The man is standing on his left foot and the woman on her right foot. Now continue with Steps 4–6, ending in a side-by-side position.

4 Man

Move back onto the right foot, leaving the left foot in place and leading the woman to dance forward across you. (Count – quick)

5 Man

Transfer your body weight forward onto the left foot, leaving the right foot in place and leading the woman to turn to the left. (Count – quick)

5 Woman

Move sideways onto the right foot, turning 90° to the left. (Count – quick)

4 Woman

Move forward onto the left foot, across the man. (Count – quick)

6 Man

Move forward, a small step, onto the right foot, starting to turn to the left. (Count – slow)

6 Woman

Continue turning and, on the right foot, make a further 180° turn to the left to end in a side-by-side position with the man on your right. Move back, a small step, onto the left foot. (Count – slow)

7 Man

Move forward onto the left foot, turning 90° to the left. (Count – quick)

7 Woman

Move back onto the right foot. (Count – quick)

8 Man

Move sideways onto the right foot, turning 90° to the left. (Count – quick)

8 Woman

Move onto the left foot, making a good step across the right foot. (Count – quick)

9 Man

Continue turning and, on the right foot, make a further 180° turn to the left and move back, a small step, onto the left foot. End in a side-by-side position with the woman on your right. (Count – slow)

9 Woman

Move forward, a small step, onto the right foot to end in a side-by-side position with the man on your left, starting to turn to the left. (Count – slow)

EL LAZO – *The name of this part of the move means the "Loop". The man completes the figure by turning the woman in a lasso-type move into a Close Contact Hold.*

10 Man

Move back, a small step, onto the right foot, leaving the left foot in place. Lead the woman to turn strongly to the left. (Count – quick)

11 Man

Transfer your body weight forward onto the left foot, leading the woman to continue turning by moving your right hand to the right over her head. (Count – quick)

12 Man

On the left foot, swivel 90° to the left and move sideways onto the right foot to end facing the woman. Circle your right hand to lead the woman to turn underneath it, concluding the move by bringing your right hand back over your own head and placing the woman's right hand on your left shoulder. (Count – slow)

12 Woman

Move forward onto the left foot, turning to the left to face the man. Close the right foot to the left foot, without weight, underneath your body. (Count – slow)

10 Woman

Move forward onto the left foot, turning 90° to the left. (Count – quick)

11 Woman

Move sideways onto the right foot, making a three-quarter turn to the left to end backing the man. (Count – quick)

Continue into the Basic Mambo or El Contro Cuerpo, resuming the appropriate hold.

El Mojito

During the rise of the Mambo through its adolescent years, the famous writer Ernest Hemingway spent much time in the *bodegas* (or bars) of Havana, imbibing, for inspiration, the rich and fruitful atmosphere of Cuba. Legend has it that the Mojito cocktail was invented for him in one of these *bodegas*. Pronounced mo – hee – to, we can apply the name to this dazzling cocktail of Mambo moves. Start in a Double Hand Hold. The man is standing on the right foot and the woman on the left foot having danced, for example, the New York.

HALF TURN TO CUDDLE POSITION

1 Man
Move back onto the left foot, leading the woman away from you and leaving the right foot in place. (Count – quick)

1 Woman
Move back onto the right foot, away from the man, leaving the left foot in place. (Count – quick)

2 Man
Transfer your body weight forward onto the right foot. Leading the woman towards your right side, raise your left hand and start to turn her to her left by moving your left hand to the right (Count – quick)

2 Woman
Transfer your body weight forward onto the left foot, starting to turn to the left. (Count – quick)

3 Man
Move forward, a small step, onto the left foot. Take your left hand over the woman's head and lower it to waist height into a "cuddle" position, with the woman ending on your right side. (Count – slow)

3 Woman
Move forward onto the right foot towards the man's right side, leaving the left foot in place. On the right foot, swivel approximately 180° to the left to end in a side-by-side position with the man on your left. (Count – slow)

LAS CARIOCAS – *In this part of the move, the man and woman move around a circle.*

4 Man

In a Cuddle Hold, move forward onto the right foot, starting to move clockwise around a circle. (Count – quick)

4 Woman

In a Cuddle Hold, move back onto the left foot, starting to move clockwise around a circle. (Count – quick)

5 Man

Move forward onto the left foot, moving clockwise around the circle. (Count – quick)

5 Woman

Move back onto the right foot, moving clockwise around the circle. (Count – quick)

6 Man

Move forward onto the right foot, moving clockwise around the circle, and tap the left foot slightly forward without weight. (Count – slow)

6 Woman

Move back onto the left foot, moving clockwise around the circle, and tap the right foot slightly forward without weight. (Count – slow)

ROLLING OFF THE ARM

7 Man

Releasing hold with your left hand, move side-ways onto the left foot, leaving the right foot in place. Lead the woman to start to roll off your right arm. (Count – quick)

7 Woman

Turning 90° to the right, move forward onto the right foot, away from the man. (Count – quick)

8 Man

Partly close the right foot towards the left foot, still leading the woman to roll off your arm. (Count – quick)

8 Woman

Turning a further 90° to the right, move sideways onto the left foot, away from the man. (Count – quick)

9 Man

Move sideways, a small step, onto the left foot, leading the woman to finish rolling off your arm. (Count – slow)

LAS QUEBRADITAS CUBANAS – *These are the "Split Cuban Breaks".*

10 Man

Move forward and across, a small step, to check onto the right foot, away from the woman, keeping the right foot pointing to the front. (Count – quick)

10 Woman

Move forward and across, a small step, to check onto the left foot, away from the man, keeping the left foot pointing to the front. (Count – quick)

9 Woman

On the left foot, pivot 180° to the right to end facing the same way as the man and move sideways onto the right foot. (Count – slow)

11 Man

Transfer your body weight back onto the left foot. (Count – quick)

11 Woman

Transfer your body weight back onto the right foot. (Count – quick)

12 Man

Move sideways, a small step, onto the right foot, towards the woman. (Count – slow)

12 Woman

Move sideways, a small step, onto the left foot, towards the man. (Count – slow)

13 Man

Move forward and across, a small step, to check onto the left foot, towards the woman, keeping the left foot pointing to the front. (Count – quick)

13 Woman

Move forward and across, a small step, to check onto the right foot, towards the man, keeping the right foot pointing to the front. (Count – quick)

14 Man

Transfer your body weight back onto the right foot. (Count – quick)

14 Woman

Transfer your body weight back onto the left foot. (Count – quick)

15 Man

Move sideways, a small step, onto the left foot, away from the woman. (Count – slow)

15 Woman

Move sideways, a small step, onto the right foot, away from the man. (Count – slow)

SPOT TURN

17 Man
Transfer your body weight forward onto the left foot. (Count – quick)

17 Woman
Transfer your body weight forward onto the right foot. (Count – quick)

16 Man
Release hold with your right hand. On the left foot, swivel 90° to the left and move forward onto the right foot, leaving the left foot in place. Once on the right foot, swivel 180° to the left to end facing the woman and with the right foot back. (Count – quick)

16 Woman
On the right foot, swivel 90° to the right and move forward onto the left foot, leaving the right foot in place. Once on the left foot, swivel 180° to the right to end with the left foot back. (Count – quick)

18 Man
Move forward onto the right foot, resuming hold. (Count – slow)

18 Woman
Move forward onto the left foot, resuming hold. (Count – slow)

Continue with your choice of hot Mambo moves.

Los Giros Locos

Here is a short but impressive move, which starts with a turn one way and then the other, hence the name, which means "the Crazy Turns". Start in a Double Hand Hold. The man is standing on the right foot and the woman on the left foot. Note the variation that can be built into the figure in Steps 7–9.

1 Man

Move back onto the left foot, leaving the right foot in place and leading the woman away from you. (Count – quick)

2 Man

Transfer your body weight onto the right foot. Leading the woman towards your right side, raise your left hand and start to turn the woman to her left by moving your left hand to the right. (Count – quick)

3 Man

Move forward, a small step, onto the left foot. Take your left hand over the woman's head and lower it to shoulder height into a Cuddle Position, with the woman ending on your right side and your right hand around her waist. (Count – slow)

1 Woman

Move back onto the right foot, away from the man, leaving the left foot in place. (Count – quick)

2 Woman

Transfer your body weight forward onto the left foot, starting to turn to the left. (Count – quick)

3 Woman

Move forward onto the right foot, towards the man's right side, leaving the left foot in place. On the right foot, swivel approximately 180° to the left to end in a side-by-side position with the man on your left. (Count – slow)

4 Man

Move back onto the right foot, leaving the left foot in place and turning approximately 90° to the right to create space for the woman. Lead the woman to dance a turn to the right in place with a firm pull of your right hand, while moving your left hand over her head. (Count – quick)

5 Man

Transfer your body weight forward onto the left foot, starting to turn to the left. Lower your left hand to waist height and raise your right hand ready to pass underneath it. (Count – quick)

6 Man

Move sideways and across onto the right foot, passing your right hand over your head and ending with both hands at waist height. (Count – slow)

4 Woman

Transfer your body weight onto the left foot, swivelling strongly in place, 180° to the right. (Count – quick)

5 Woman

Move forward onto the right foot, turning to the right and moving around the back of the man. (Count – quick)

6 Woman

Move sideways onto the left foot, ending on the man's left side. (Count – slow)

CHANGING SIDES – *Once you have danced Steps 7–9, you can repeat them in the opposite direction using the opposite foot, then again in the original direction and with the original foot, in which case, you are dancing the Beach Blanket.*

7 Man

Move back, a small step, onto the left foot, leaving the right foot in place. (Count – quick)

8 Man

Transfer your body weight forward onto the right foot. (Count – quick)

9 Man

Move sideways onto the left foot, across the woman. (Count – slow)

9 Woman

Move sideways onto the right foot, across and behind the man, ending on his right side a little behind him. (Count – slow)

7 Woman

Move forward, a small step, onto the right foot, leaving the left foot in place. (Count – quick)

8 Woman

Transfer your body weight back onto the left foot. (Count – quick)

EXIT

10 Man

Release hold with your right hand and move back onto the right foot, leaving the left foot in place and leading the woman forward with your left hand. (Count – quick)

11 Man

Transfer your body weight forward onto the left foot, still leading the woman forward. End by leading the woman to swivel sharply to her left to face you. (Count – quick)

12 Man

Move forward onto the right foot. (Count – slow)

12 Woman

Move back onto the left foot. (Count – slow)

11 Woman

Move forward onto the right foot, leaving the left foot in place. On the right foot, swivel to the left to face the man. (Count – quick)

10 Woman

Move forward onto the left foot. (Count – quick)

Continue with your favourite Mambo move.

Los Giros Frenados

Los Giros Frenados (or the "Checked Turns") show how a relatively simple figure can be developed into something far more adventurous and spectacular. Try the move first without hand hold, then add the holds and arm movements as you become familiar with the pattern. Start in a Double Hand Hold. The man is standing on the right foot and the woman on the left foot.

1 Man
Move sideways onto the left foot, leaving the right foot in place. Lead the woman to turn to the left by moving your left hand to the right and over her head, ending by lowering your hand to waist height.
(Count – quick)

2 Man
Transfer your body weight sideways onto the right foot, leading the woman to turn back to the right with a gentle pull of your right hand and raising your left hand over her head.
(Count – quick)

3 Man
Close the left foot to the right foot in an open facing position.
(Count – slow)

3 Woman
On the left foot, swivel 180° to the right and move sideways, a small step, onto the right foot. (Count – slow)

4–6 Man & Woman
Dance Steps 4–6 of the Basic Mambo in Double Hand Hold. (Counts – quick, quick, slow)

1 Woman
On the left foot, swivel 180° to the left and move sideways onto the right foot in a Cucuracha-type move. (Count – quick)

2 Woman
Transfer your body weight onto the left foot. (Count – quick)

Merengue – an Introduction

The Merengue (pronounced me-rren-gay) has now established itself as one of the most popular Latin American dances. It comes from the Dominican Republic in the Caribbean, which has become a favourite holiday destination in recent years. The mood of the Merengue reflects that holiday atmosphere and, since the rhythm and steps could not be simpler, demand for it in Latin clubs and dance schools continues to grow and grow. The music of the Merengue is lively and is popular even with people who do not dance it. One of the top artists responsible for the best Merengue music is Juan Luis Guerra and his band 4.40. His hits "La Bilirrubina" and "El Costo de la Vida" have become Merengue standards.

The Merengue beat is a strong one-two rhythm, which is interpreted as two dance steps using the characteristic pumping action of the Merengue. There are no deviations from this simple rhythm so the steps themselves are very easy – an advantage which has resulted in many people being able to get up and just dance the Merengue without any formal tuition. If you can walk, you can Merengue. The dance does not progress around the floor but remains very much on the spot, with the man leading his partner to dance a variety of very gentle, slow turning moves, usually over eight steps. More expert dancers may spice up their Merengue by dancing the moves over just four steps. It is how these turns are put together plus the fabulous music that provide much of the enjoyment of Merengue.

MERENGUE ACTION

Most of the steps use the characteristic Merengue action. On the first step, the foot is placed in position with pressure onto the floor through the inside edge of the ball of the foot but the body weight is not transferred onto the foot. On the second step, the body weight is transferred onto the foot that has just been placed while releasing the heel of the other foot from the floor and allowing the knee of that leg to move a little across the knee of the standing leg. The Merengue Action feels a little like a pumping movement, but it should not be exaggerated. The steps of the Merengue are usually danced with the feet a little apart.

Left: The lively Merengue is a favourite all over the world and the simplicity of the basic steps makes it easy to learn.

Basic Merengue

The basic one-two rhythm of Merengue music makes the steps very simple – in a way, rather like marking time. You will find yourself enjoying the infectious Merengue beat in no time. Start in a Close Contact Hold with the man standing on the right foot and the woman on the left foot. Importantly, the Merengue Action is used.

1 Man
Step in place with the left foot. (Count – slow)

1 Woman
Step in place with the right foot. (Count – slow)

Style Tip

As you dance the Merengue, the look and feel of your dancing will be considerably enhanced by keeping the upper part of your body as still as possible and focusing all the Merengue Action into the legs, which will result in a seductively attractive hip movement.

2 Man
Step in place with the right foot. (Count – slow)

2 Woman
Step in place with tne left foot. (Count – slow)

3–8 Man & Woman
Repeat Steps 1–2 up to the count of eight.

The Merengue Basic can be repeated and gradually rotated in either direction over the eight counts.

MERENGUE MELT-DOWN

The Merengue Melt-Down is not so much a figure in itself as an embellishment of the Basic Merengue.

Left: To dance this fun move, flex your knees and sink down to an almost sitting position before rising again to normal height as you dance the Basic Merengue. During the Melt-Down, the couple may rotate the Basic Merengue.

Left: When the party really gets going, a dancer may perform the Melt-Down while leaning back like a Limbo dancer and "shimmying".

SEPARATION TO DOUBLE HAND HOLD

Many Merengue moves start with a Double Hand Hold. To move into this hold, the man simply eases the woman away from him, allowing his right hand to slide down her left arm to take up the Double Hand Hold. During the "Separation", carry on dancing the Basic Merengue, gradually moving backwards away from each other as you change hold. The Separation should last the usual eight counts.

Double Hand Hold

Left Hand to Right Hand Hold

Right Hand to Right Hand

Merengue Side Steps

Y ou can dance the Merengue Side Steps in either a Close Contact Hold or a Double Hand Hold. This figure moves first to the man's left and then to his right. To start, the man is standing on the right foot and the woman on the left foot. Remember to use the Merengue Action to give these simple steps extra style.

1 Man
Move sideways, a small step, onto the left foot. (Count – slow)

1 Woman
Move sideways, a small step, onto the right foot. (Count – slow)

2 Man
Close the right foot to the left foot. (Count – slow)

2 Woman
Close the left foot to the right foot. (Count – slow)

3–4 Man & Woman
Repeat Steps 1–2. (Counts – slow, slow)

5–8 Man
Step in place with the left foot. Move sideways, a small step, onto the right foot. Close the left foot to the right foot. Move sideways, a small step, onto the right foot. (Counts – slow, slow, slow, slow)

5–8 Woman
Step in place with the right foot. Move sideways, a small step, onto the left foot. Close the right foot to the left foot. Move sideways, a small step, onto the left foot. (Counts – slow, slow, slow, slow)

Gosh! Wowee! Yikes!

It is not uncommon for a male Latin dancer to unexpectedly express his enjoyment of the dance with a sudden outburst of "Si, Señor!", "Asi!", "Es!", "Eso!" or some other comment of satisfaction. If your partner suddenly makes some such exclamation, don't be alarmed, just carry on with the fun.

Copy-Cat Turn

In this typical Merengue move, the man leads the woman to dance a turn underneath their joined hands, then the man copies the woman. Start in a Double Hand Hold. As usual, the man is standing on the right foot and the woman on the left foot. Continue dancing the Basic Merengue steps as you turn. During Steps 1–8, the man remains facing in the same direction, while the woman turns. During Steps 9–16, the woman remains facing in the same direction, while the man turns.

1–2 Man
Bring your hands together and swing them down and over to your left as an indication to the woman that she is about to be turned.

1–2 Woman
The man will bring your hands together and swing them to your right. This is your lead that he is about to turn you to the left.

3–8 Man
Continue to dance the Basic Merengue steps facing the woman. Circle your hands, still together, anticlockwise above head height (shown left), returning them to waist height by count 8. Your hands are now crossed.

3–8 Woman
Continue to dance the Basic Merengue steps, turning anticlockwise to end facing the man on count 8.

9–15 Man

Continue to dance the Basic Merengue steps. Turn clockwise, circling your joined hands, still together, above head height and down again to waist height.

9–15 Woman

Continue to dance the Basic Merengue steps facing the man, allowing him to turn in front of you.

Leading Tip

Note that the lead for the turn initially moves in the opposite direction to the turn, suggesting that the man leads the woman by creating some turning momentum through his arms and swinging her into the turn. Having understood this convention, it is not then necessary to use any forceful swinging action in the arms or to pull the woman in any way.

16 Man

End facing the woman.

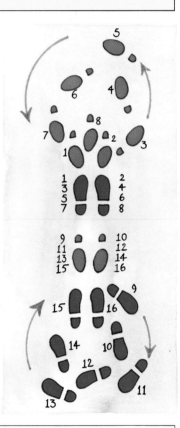

16 Woman

End with your hands at waist height.

You can now dance the Copy-Cat Turn again or continue into any other Merengue move. A popular alternative ending to the Copy-Cat Turn is La Yunta.

La Yunta

La Yunta, or "the Yoke", is a slick, suave and seductive conclusion to the Copy-Cat Turn. To create the best effect, dance the complete Copy-Cat Turn, then repeat Steps 1–8, but this time, leave the joined hands above the woman's head. The woman's arms now resemble a yoke, hence the name of this impressive move.

1–8 Man & Woman

The man releases hold with his right hand, and using only his left hand, he moves the woman's still joined hands over his own head and places them on the back of his neck, resuming close contact.

9–16 Man & Woman

Over these eight counts, the man takes the woman's right hand in his left hand and…

…the couple gradually resume a Close Contact Hold.

You can return to your programme with any of the basic Merengue moves, but a particularly good one to dance here is Steps 1–3 of La Cucuracha (described in the Mambo section of the book) with a Melt-Down action, before continuing with Steps 4–8 of the Basic Merengue.

El Barco Latino

This is a favourite figure among many *Merengueros*. Its name refers to the floating restaurant and night club in which it is often practised. Start in a Double Hand Hold with the man standing on the right foot and the woman on the left foot. Dance the Basic Merengue steps throughout this popular combination.

1–4 Man & Woman

Making a 90° turn to the left, raise your hands. The man lowers his left hand over his own head to end on his left shoulder and his right hand over the woman's head to end with her left hand on her left shoulder. The man's right arm will end across the top of the woman's back.

5–8 Man & Woman

In this position, walk forward four steps around a circle. The man starts with the left foot and the woman with the right foot. Steps 5–8 can be repeated, in which case this part of the move is called the Revolving Door.

9–12 Man & Woman

Raise both hands and hold them together. The man dances four steps on the spot while the woman continues to walk forward around the man's back, ending opposite the man's left side. The man starts with the left foot and the woman with the right foot.

13–16 Man & Woman

Your hands are now crossed. The man dances four steps on the spot, while circling his hand clockwise to turn the woman to her right to end in a facing position. The man starts with the left foot and the woman with the right foot.

> *Continue with any Merengue move.*

La Silla Giratoria

La Silla Giratoria ("the Swivel Chair") introduces a new feel to your Merengue and is an excellent figure to enjoy when you are dancing on a crowded floor. The woman dances a series of swivels around the man as the move rotates steadily anticlockwise. Start in Close Contact Hold with the man standing on the right foot and the woman on the left foot. Don't forget to use the Merengue Action throughout the move.

1 Man
Step in place with the left foot. (Count – slow)

2 Man
Move sideways onto the right foot, turning a little to the left to lead the woman to swivel to her right. (Count – slow)

1 Woman
Step in place with the right foot. (Count – slow)

2 Woman
On the right foot, swivel to the right to end at a right angle to the man, and place the left foot forward, a small step. (Count – slow)

3 Man

Close the left foot to the right foot, leading the woman to face you.
(Count – slow)

4 Man

Move sideways onto the right foot, turning a little to the left to lead the woman to swivel to her right. (Count – slow)

5–7 Man & Woman

Repeat Steps 1–3. (Counts – slow, slow, slow)

8 Man

Step in place with the right foot.
(Count – slow)

4 Woman

On the right foot, swivel to the right to end at a right angle to the man, and place the left foot forward, a small step.
(Count – slow)

8 Woman

Transfer your body weight onto the left foot and end facing the man.
(Count – slow)

3 Woman

Transfer your body weight onto the left foot and swivel to the left to face the man, placing the right foot slightly forward. (Count – slow)

Style Tip

For the woman, the turn to face the man will be a little sharper than the turn away from him. Some women choose to dance the step with the left foot with a short kicking action. Try it when you feel comfortable with the move.

Las Miradas Dobles

Las Miradas Dobles, meaning "the Double Take", is one of the few moves that deviate from the standard Merengue rhythm, making it an excellent faster move to add a little spice when the dance hots up. In this move, borrowed from the Cha Cha Cha, the Merengue Action is not used. Start in a Double Hand Hold with the man standing on the right foot and the woman on the left foot.

1 Man
On the right foot, swivel 45° to the left and move forward, a small step, onto the left foot. (Count – slow)

2 Man
On the left foot, swivel 90° to the right and move forward, a small step, onto the right foot. (Count – slow)

3 Man
On the right foot, swivel 90° to the left and move forward, a small step, onto the left foot. (Count – quick)

1 Woman
On the left foot, swivel 45° to the right and move forward, a small step, onto the right foot. (Count – slow)

2 Woman
On the right foot, swivel 90° to the left and move forward, a small step, onto the left foot. (Count – slow)

3 Woman
On the left foot, swivel 90° to the right and move forward, a small step, onto the right foot. (Count – quick)

4 Man

Almost close the right foot to the left foot. (Count – quick)

5 Man

Move forward, a small step, onto the left foot. (Count – slow)

4 Woman

Almost close the left foot to the right foot. (Count – quick)

5 Woman

Move forward, a small step, onto the right foot. (Count – slow)

6–10 Man

On the left foot, swivel 90° to the right and move forward, a small step, onto the right foot. On the right foot, swivel 90° to the left and move forward, a small step, onto the left foot. On the left foot, swivel 45° to the right and move forward, a small step, onto the right foot. Almost close the left foot to the right foot. Move sideways, a small step, onto the right foot and end facing the woman. (Counts – slow, slow, quick, quick, slow)

6–10 Woman

On the right foot, swivel 90° to the left and move forward, a small step, onto the left foot. On the left foot, swivel 90° to the right and move forward, a small step, onto the right foot. On the right foot, swivel 45° to the left and move forward, a small step, onto the left foot. Almost close the right foot to the left foot. Move sideways, a small step, onto the left foot and end facing the man. (Counts – slow, slow, quick, quick, slow)

Turns

Merengue is all to do with the action and turns, so let's have a look at some more of the standard Merengue turns. As usual, in the following turns, the man starts with the left foot and the woman with the right foot. The turns can be danced over four or eight counts, depending on how they fit in with other moves.

HALF TURN TO THE LEFT

In the Half Turn to the Left, the man raises his left hand, while keeping his right hand at waist height. The man then leads the woman to turn by moving his left hand to the right. By Step 8, the woman will have turned left into the man's right arm on his right side. To exit, simply reverse the process to a further eight counts.

HALF TURN TO THE RIGHT

In the Half Turn to the Right, the man raises his right hand, while keeping his left hand at waist height. The man then leads the woman to turn by moving his right hand to the left. By Step 8, the woman will have turned right into the man's left arm on his left side. To exit, reverse the process to a further eight counts.

ARMLOCK TURN TO THE LEFT

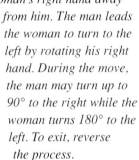

In the Armlock Turn to the Left, the man raises his right hand, while keeping his left hand at waist height and pressing the woman's right hand away from him. The man leads the woman to turn to the left by rotating his right hand. During the move, the man may turn up to 90° to the right while the woman turns 180° to the left. To exit, reverse the process.

ARMLOCK TURN TO THE RIGHT

In the Armlock Turn to the Right, the man raises his left hand, while keeping his right hand at waist height and pressing the woman's left hand away from him. The man leads the woman to turn to the right by rotating his left hand. During the move, the man may turn up to 90° to the left while the woman turns 180° to the right. To exit, reverse the process.

Combining the Turns

Half Turn to the Left with Armlock Turn to the Right
Dance the Half Turn to the Left over eight steps, then exit over four, ensuring that the woman is facing the man by the end of Step 12. His left hand is still raised and his right hand is still at waist height. The man now leads the Armlock Turn to the Right over four steps to finish by Step 16. Exit as normal.

Half Turn to the Right with Armlock Turn to the Left
Dance the Half Turn to the Right over eight steps, then exit over four, ensuring that the woman is facing the man by the end of Step 12. His right hand is still raised and his left hand is still at waist height. The man now leads the Armlock Turn to the Left over four steps to finish by Step 16. Exit as normal.

El Nudo

Not the "Nude" but the "Knot", this title accurately describes the fun you might have as you learn to solve the challenge of getting into and out of this more advanced move. To dance El Nudo, start in a Double Hand Hold with the man standing on the right foot and the woman on the left foot.

17–20
Man & Woman
The man now leads the woman towards him and behind his back as he takes his left hand over his head and gradually turns on the spot to the right to face the woman.

1–8 Man & Woman
Dance the Armlock Turn to the Right over eight steps, but this time with the man turning 180° on the spot to the right, lifting his right hand over his head to end back to back with the woman on his left.

9–12 Man & Woman
Move to the left to end with each partner on the right of the other, still back to back.

13–16 Man & Woman
Reverse Steps 9–12 by moving to the right, still back to back. The man raises his left arm over the woman's head by Step 16.

21–28 Man & Woman
By keeping his left hand raised, the man leads the woman into a Half Turn to the Right on the spot over four steps. Releasing hold with the right hand, the man now turns the woman on the spot underneath his left hand, before resuming a Double Hand Hold.

Steps 25–28 can be danced without resuming Double Hand Hold and then repeated before finally taking up the Double Hand Hold, or Close Contact Hold if you prefer.

Music Suggestions

MAMBO

Slower Mambos for beginners:

"Mambo No. 5", "Mambo No. 8" and "Mambo Jambo" by Pérez Prado are all classics with a slower tempo ideal for practising your moves.

"Guaglione" by Pérez Prado shot to No. 1 in the UK charts in 1996. It is a catchy tune with an ideal tempo for new *Mamberos* to practise to.

"Mambo Suavecito" by Tito Puente and his Orchestra has a great rhythmic feel and a steady tempo which is great to dance to while you are building up your programme.

"Tatalibaba" is a timeless Mambo classic by Tito Puente and his Orchestra. The steady rhythm and comfortable tempo make it a super track for dancers.

Faster Mambos for more practised dancers:

"Lupita", written by Pérez Prado but performed by Fruko y Orchesta, is a more modern version of a Mambo classic ideal to enjoy once you have practised the moves.

"Ran Kan Kan" is a favourite among *Mamberos* as it has a lot of drive and is one to enjoy as the temperature rises and the atmosphere reaches melt-down point. The version by Tito Puente and his Orchestra is especially good.

"Mambo Inn" by Tito Puente and his Orchestra combines the Big Band sound with a hot Latin rhythm and tempo. When

you have practised your moves to slower numbers, try them to the more common tempo of this Mambo standard.

MERENGUE

"Mas Que Amiga", performed by Grupo Bananas, is a romantic Merengue that captures perfectly the holiday feel of the dance. It is played at a steady tempo ideal for practising.

"El Tiburon" by Proyecto Uno is a Latin club mega-favourite Merengue. It is a little suggestive and has a fabulous, strong beat and a chorus that everyone joins in, making it as addictive a Merengue as you will find. Very highly recommended.

"A Gozar Todo el Mundo" by Banda la Bocana is a good example of Latin "House" music, which can also be enjoyed for Merengue in many Latin clubs. The pace is steady and not too fast.

"Las Mujeres" by Sergio Vargas is a club favourite with a lot of drive, and like all good Merengue music, it has a fantastic rhythm. This one is not too fast and is highly recommended.

"El Costo de la Vida" and "La Bilirrubina": top Latin star Juan Luis Guerra is always popular among *Merengueros*, and these two Merengue hits are among his best, guaranteed to get you onto the floor.

As you build up your fluency through practice, you will want to try a slightly faster pace of Merengue, such as the excellent "Mujeres Calientes" by Hermanos Rosario.

Most clubs seem to include one very fast fun Merengue in their evening's programme. Typical of such manic Merengues are "La Cosquillita" by the universally popular Juan Luis Guerra, "Coqueta y Sabrosa" by Zafra Negra, and "De Risitas" by Eddy Herrera.

Further Information

It is to be hoped that this introduction has given you a taste of the Mambo and Merengue and has whetted your appetite to learn more of the fascinating and enjoyable dances and rhythms from Latin America. With the moves you have learned in this book, you will soon be out on the floor dancing and enjoying the hot Latin American rhythm of the Mambo and Merengue. Why not join others who share your interest and who are just as keen as you are to learn more? Look up your local dance school or call a Latin club in your area. There is no substitute for getting out there and doing it. Your teacher will be able to give you personal guidance to help you refine your technique, and you will be surprised by how quickly you progress. Remember that most people find dancing a little difficult at first, but given a little time, patience, perseverance and practice, you will soon have learned to dance, which is a lifetime's reward for such a little investment.

ACKNOWLEDGEMENTS
Many of the sequences in this book feature Three Times Undefeated Dutch Professional Latin American Champions and world-class dancers, Harm-Jan Schadenberg and Wendy Kroeze, whose help we gratefully acknowledge. The author and publishers would also like to thank the following for their participation in the photography of this book: Luís Bittencourt, Berg Dias, Tanya Janes, Karina Padilha Rebelo and Mina di Placido. Their expertise and enthusiasm were invaluable.